HOW TO
IMPROVE YOUR HANDWRITING

Martin Good

NATIONAL EXTENSION COLLEGE

The author
Martin Good is Head of the Basic Skills Unit at the
National Extension College. Formerly staff tutor
for Special Adult Learning Programmes in Bedford-
shire. Also worked in the prison education service
and taught in further education colleges. Co-author
of *How's It Going? An Alternative to Testing Students in Adult Literacy, Second Chances 1983* and
Basic Education 16-99 (NEC 1981)

CONTENTS

Part 1: **Introduction**

Down to earth

I am not a handwriting specialist. In fact, my own writing is rather bad, though I'm glad to say my own methods are improving it! But that's one reason why I understand so well the problems of bad writers. We all *know* we write badly and we've probably been given large helpings of advice on how to improve. But we just don't ever get round to it. Or we start on writing patterns, italics, whatever, but don't get very far.

That takes me to the reason I've written this book. Handwriting is an area of work which has been left too much to handwriting specialists. Now there's nothing wrong with specialists. But nearly all of them are concerned with teaching children, or people who have never tried to write before. They always seem to want you to start at the beginning (one might say 'from scratch')! And that's why so many of us fail; starting 'from scratch' is always a tempting idea, but it's actually a very bad principle for adult learning. I am writing this as a teacher of adults. That means I am aiming at busy people who need a practical, down-to-earth method for improving a skill they already have. Not by 'starting again', but by starting from where they are and building from there — a method that doesn't pretend to change you completely but allows improvements to 'seep in' to your normal writing as time goes by; a method that focuses your attention on what you're doing in a way that helps you improve yourself. The idea is to take away the mystery, the dream of becoming a perfect writer, and bring it all down to earth. So you won't find any writing patterns at all in this book. The nearest to that are the letter formations on p. 21. But like everything else in this book, you can take them or leave them and either way your writing will probably improve, if you work at it.

In the first part of the book I will look at some of the feelings you may have about your handwriting. The idea is to help you get a clear idea of how much you want it to change, and what you eventually want it to be. The rest of the book is all practical activities. Instructions on how to do them are on page 21.

To help you through Part 1 there are questions every now and again, called Activities. When you come to one I'd like you to stop and think, perhaps write your thoughts down, perhaps talk to someone else about them. (More about that later.)

Here's the first:

What do you like about your handwriting?
What don't you like about it?
What do you think you could do to get it the way you want it?
What help or support do you need from other people?

You could write the answers down in a list as has been done here:

- I don't like anything about it.
- I don't like the fact that no-one can read it.
- I'd love to work at it - maybe write slower?
- Perhaps other people could learn to read it!

What is a 'good writer'?

Often people who want to learn something are put off learning it by their own impatience. You have in your head an idea of what it's like to be able to do it perfectly; you know you aren't anywhere near as good as that. So you get discouraged.

But you're probably wrong about what a good writer is, and what he does. He almost certainly *doesn't* write superbly, straight off. (The only people I've met who can do that are primary school teachers. Perhaps that's why we all get such a complex about it so young!) A good writer writes clearly and legibly *when he has to*. When he doesn't have to he probably writes as fast as he can, and as long as he can read it, he's not worried. In fact, most good writers make fair copies of what they write. If they didn't they probably wouldn't be good writers.

So are you a good writer after all? Someone who can make reasonably fair copies if they have to?

Well, carry on reading anyhow, as there may still be something useful in the book, even so!

What is your first memory about learning to write?
Do you think the way you were taught has any bearing on how and what you think of your handwriting now?
If so, what?

Here's what Debbie said:

My first memory is of my hand aching because I was clut-ching my pencil much too tightly.

Then we had to do pages of boring exercises that did not look like ~~these~~ letters and I couldn't see the point of them.

When we could write lightly enough with a pencil we were allowed to use an ink pen. I was the only one in the class who was still using a pencil and I was teased about it.

Does this bring back any memories?

Why does bad handwriting matter?

Bad handwriting is very like bad spelling in the way people talk about it. Sometimes you get the feeling that everyone wrote beautifully in the good old days, and that bad handwriting only came in with permissiveness and colour TV. Sometimes you'd think it's a sign of laziness, dishonesty or lack of consideration for the reader. And sometimes it's another sign of the collapse of our education system, along with the three Rs and good table manners.

It's almost never seen as a skill which some people are better at than others. For some reason we are all supposed to be equally good at it, even though everyone knows that everyone is different. My guess is that it all starts at school, where so many of us get into trouble or lose marks for bad handwriting.

We bad writers get an inferiority complex about it; good writers become ridiculously snooty about it. And the division of the population into these two groups lasts for the rest of our lives. A few lucky ones escape the normal disapproval; one wonders how many doctors choose their profession *because* they write so badly?

And yet, when all the snobbery and other nonsense is cleared away, handwriting does matter. Of course it does. The reader has got to be able to understand what the writer is telling him. Even typists must be able to read their drafts. And it's much more enjoyable to read something that's handwritten so well that you don't have to keep stopping to puzzle it out.

Do you like getting handwritten letters?
How much does it worry you if they're untidy or hard to read?
Do you disapprove of the person who has written untidily?
How does other people's writing affect you?

Most people handwrite their letters. If those are written legibly it's an added bonus (though it's nice getting letters even if you can't read them). And I for one prefer to get personal letters in handwriting because handwriting is individual. You can tell who's written to you just by glancing at the envelope. And familiar handwriting brings someone closer to you somehow; even if we can't all work out each other's personalities from handwriting (as graphologists claim to do), we do express something of ourselves in it, and the reader picks that up, whatever it is, and uses it to help bring our words to life.

A final note on why it matters: people (especially youngsters) are frequently told by teachers, careers' officers and other helpful souls that letters to employers should be perfectly spelled and beautifully written. Undoubtedly this is true for some employers; I have a feeling, though, that it's not true for all of them. I have letters and tapes of people who are actually suspicious of potential employees who write (or even talk) too well. It all depends on the job you want! Real life is always more complicated than one would wish. Even good handwriting is not *always* a good thing.

What were the good things about the way you were taught?
Do you think the people who taught you could have done better; If so try to imagine the scene as you would have liked it. It's probably a good idea to do this by talking to someone about it.

Here's what Anna said:

Nothing was good. First of all I was made to change from my left hand to my right but my parents stopped them after 2 weeks. Then I went to a school that did italic handwriting. Italic pens for left-handed people have a funny bent nib so the ink never gets to the end. And they were always nagging me to put my paper straight. If you're left-handed you've got to put the paper sideways or you can't see what you're doing.

I would have liked them to be sensible enough to know that I had to put my paper sideways. Any teacher who doesn't realise that is stupid.

I wish I had learnt italic because I think it looks really good, but I couldn't.

Childish and mature writing

A lot of people worry about their handwriting being childish. Normally they mean that it's obvious that they write very slowly and painstakingly. Perhaps they don't join up the letters. One of my students whose writing was bad was told to slow down to make it clearer. The result was that her writing looked more 'childish'.

Milkman

2 pints today please

Adult or mature handwriting is fast. It's often not all that clear, especially if you try to read it word by word. But the main characteristic that
distinguishes mature writing from childish writing is speed. Ways of
speeding up are included on p. 24.

What pen should you use?

When I was at school everyone looked down on biros and we had to use
dip-pens. Nowadays almost everyone uses biros; I would only recommend
buying an expensive pen to people who don't lose things! Otherwise it's
not worth it. Use whatever you have to hand. If you've not written much
before, try out different ones — felt-tips, biros, ball-tips, etc. When you
find one you like, use that. If you are buying a pen, spend some time in
the shop trying out different nibs. Choose the one you like best, that feels
best. And you'll also have to decide whether to go for an ink cartridge
(fine till you run out and haven't got a new one on you) or a pen that fills
from a bottle (no good if you tend to spill things).

Do you like using biros, pens, felt-tips, etc?
Which is your favourite?
What do you like and dislike about each?

What should your writing be like?

In all work with adults who are *worried* about not knowing something,
the greatest problem is always: How do you know when you're OK? In
this case: What should your writing be like?

Like this?

Dear Martin,

Thanks for your note. I enclose proofs of your book and await your comments and corrections.

Or this?

Dear Martin,

I'm sorry I didn't receive your letter until Friday. Will Tuesday do?

Or this?

Dear Martin,

The books you ordered on your last visit here have now arrived. I'll bring them with me when I come to your office on Thursday.

Or this?

If you would like to explore this (we could actually hold and open for a consultancy) or just to generally talk it over, why not come here & see what we do & how we work?

Yours

L

All those are examples of handwriting in letters I have received at my office. They are all perfectly legible, though you wouldn't recognise, say, n as ~ or o as • if you had to decipher each letter. Luckily you usually don't have to do that. You recognise writing through understanding the meaning of what's on the page, not by interpreting each individual letter. That's a very important point, because no one could read handwriting at all if it weren't true. Your brain can translate hot *hot* HOT *hot* *hot* all into the same word. All readers have the ability to recognise meanings from a great range of clues. You have to be able to read enough of the letters to piece together the sense, but you don't have to read each one. So your writing should be clear enough for that. Which means that your tall letters — *l, t,* etc. should be noticeably tall; your *g*s and *p*s and *y*s should have tails that can be seen; your *t*s should be crossed, etc. The point is — contrasts must be noticeable. Contrasts between tall and short, round and straight, etc. Not perfect, just noticeable.

Your handwriting should also be part of you. It shouldn't be like anyone else's; it's your handwriting, so it's your personality. It *is* you. You can't avoid that, so make the best of it!

Do you have different moods about your handwriting style?
If so, what are they?

Here's what Jane said:

> I write small and neat~~ly~~ when writing letters of importance.
> If I'm in a hurry my writing becomes rushed.
> When I'm taking messages my writing is messy and large.

> I start off writing small and neat but the quicker my thoughts come, the quicker I write and the untidier it gets.

Handwriting and spelling
Good fast handwriting is an advantage for people wanting to improve their spelling. If your hand is fluent and confident you can teach it to spell

some things for you. They will just flow out of your pen.

One side-effect of using this book, for people worried about spelling, will be that you'll learn to spell 100 words with confidence and they are the most common words in the language. They make up over half of what most people write!

How to use this book

First, there are four questions to help you decide how to start on your writing. Each question leads you to a particular section of the book which deals with one aspect of the problem. Each section helps you to notice your own particular difficulties and suggests ways to work on them and ways to organise your practice. The idea is really to help you concentrate your own problem-solving ability on your handwriting. What I hope will happen is that you realise early on that you know all the time how to do it yourself; that it's really so simple that you couldn't see it for looking. (But not till *after* you've bought the book!)

Get help from someone!

It'll be much easier, and more enjoyable, if you get someone to work with you. Either you can both work on your handwriting together or you can simply use your companion as someone to talk to, do the activities with, share ideas. If there isn't one person, use several, a bit at a time. Ask them some of the questions I've asked you. Turn the conversation to handwriting and see what they feel about it. If they're snobs, tell them so!

How long will it take?

It depends what you mean by 'it'. If you follow the advice in the book you'll probably see an improvement within days. But all learning is like that. It starts quickly, falls off into a slow period, zooms ahead again, etc. Even if you practise for the same amount of time every day, what you achieve varies enormously. And I don't expect you to do it like that, though you can. For most people practice is more haphazard. Sometimes there's time, sometimes not. But that hasn't answered the question, 'how long?' The answer is; I don't know. But give yourself three months before you check your progress. (To see how to do that, read the section on the 'check' pages.) Then if you want to carry on, it's up to you.

How long do you think it will take?
How long do you want it to take?
How much practice can you fit in? How often?

Are you left-handed?

If so, you may well feel that handwriting in English was designed by some-one who hates left-handed people. And you're right, in a way. The system is not suitable for you, so it's much harder to do it quickly and legibly. But it's not impossible. There's no need to try and force yourself to be right-handed. Indeed, a lot of people whose teachers did that to them are still suffering, years later. At worst, the effect is to prevent someone from learning to read and write properly, *ever*. At best, you'll be left with a nasty, painful memory. Most likely is that you'll have a hang-up about writing for the rest of your life.

All the exercises in this book will work for you too, though it may take a bit longer to speed up. You must also make sure you find a good angle to write from. The paper should be in the right position for your pen. Most left-handers angle it so that they're almost writing from top to bot-tom instead of from side to side. This picture shows a typical left-handed writing position:

But, as I've emphasised about everything in this book, do it your own way. Be comfortable. If you've got a position which you're used to and prefer, don't change it completely just because I say so. Try out different ones, see which are best and then do the exercises. There's no magic in the position of your paper — the magic is in practising and taking notice of what you're doing.

The 'check' pages

Pages 17, 18 and 19 of this book are blank. On p. 17 write a short passage in your quickest, sloppiest hand, then copy out the same passage again in your neatest hand. Time yourself each time and write down the date and how long it took. After three months do another piece of sloppy writing on p. 18, and again copy it out neatly. Time and date them. Compare them with your earlier efforts. After another three months do it again, and carry on every three months till you decide to stop. When you run out of pages in this book, keep your own record in an exercise book. If you can't think of what to write, put down the words of 'God Save the Queen', 'Eskimo Nell', or anything you know by heart.

Here's an example:

The Independent Broadcasting Authority (IBA), based in London, is responsible for both Independent Television and Radio. It doesn't make its own programmes or own any stations.

The Independent Broadcasting Authority (IBA), based in London, is responsible for both Independent Television and Radio. It doesn't make its own programmes or own any stations.

Self-test 1

Writing quickly

Date:

Time taken:

Writing neatly

Date:

Time taken:

Self-test 2 (after three months)

Writing quickly

Date:

Time taken:

Writing neatly

Date:

Time taken:

Writing quickly

Date:

Time taken:

Writing neatly

Date:

Time taken:

The method

The basic idea is that you learn to write certain important words well, one or two at a time. The words included here are mainly 'structure' words — that is, words which are used a lot in our language to make it flow. Words like 'the', 'and', 'is', 'when', etc. One hundred of them make up over half the words we read, it's said. So obviously they also make up over half the words we write. I have also included common words involved in letter-writing: 'Dear', 'sincerely', and the months. And you can list particular words you want to work on as well. The golden rule of the method — and of all adult education — is that you take it at your own speed, in your own way. Just do one or two words at a time (one a day, one a week — whatever works out best) and let the improvement SEEP INTO your normal writing. The practice you do on one word won't only affect that word; you'll start to *notice* things about other, similar words you're writing. Improving 'and' will also improve 'sand', 'band', 'land', 'grand'. You'll find you start to notice for yourself many of the things that writing patterns teach you, e.g. the importance of tallness for tall letters like **b** and **l** , clear roundishness for the round bit of **a** and straightishness for the straight bit. *Noticing* and then practising is really what it's all about. I call this method proof-*writing*. Proof-*reading* is a skill which mainly involves noticing the way words are spelled, whether punctuation is OK, etc. in books that are soon to be printed. The proof-reader deliberately makes himself aware of aspects of reading that most of us ignore. But it's an unhappy proof-reader who does it all the time, because he can no longer enjoy reading normally.

I want you to develop the same kind of awareness about your writing, but *not to do it too much*. At all costs you must *not* let this business of improving your writing become a burden that makes you hate doing it. Become aware, but only of a *few things at a time*. Be slow. Most of the time just carry on exactly as before. It'll all build up fast enough without being in a hurry.

The questions

1. Can you write at all (that is, form all the letters)? If so, go on to question 2. If not, turn to p. 21.

2. Do you write fairly fluently? Or slowly and painstakingly? If it's fairly fluent, go on to question 3. If it's slow, turn to p. 24.

3. Do you get mixed up between capitals and small letters? If yes, turn to p. 29. If no, go on to question 4.

4. You write fairly quickly but rather badly. Go on to p. 32.

Each of these questions directs you to a different starting point. But you'll find that you are referred backwards and forwards in the book quite a lot, as many of the techniques I suggest are useful for different problems. So it's not a bad idea to scan through the whole lot now, to get an idea of the whole approach.

Part 2: **If you can't write at all**

Below, and on p. 22, you'll find all the letters in the alphabet, once in lower case (small), once in UPPER CASE (big). You'll need to learn to do both. The small ones are more important; most of our writing is in lower case, probably because it's faster. Page 29 tells you when to use upper case letters correctly. I've also included all the numbers; you'll need them for dates, addresses and so on.

The arrows are meant to show you where to start and how to carry on with each letter. Practise only a few at a time — as many as you can do without too much sweat.

First, go over them with the forefinger of the hand you write with. That's called finger-tracing. It helps you get the feel of the letter and of the movements you have to make; you get a sense of rhythm for each letter you're working on. Start slowly, then speed up when you've got the movement right. Here's a routine to follow. You'll find you've very soon passed on to Part 5.

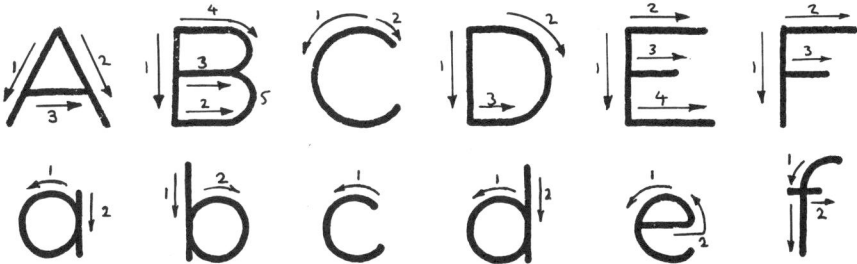

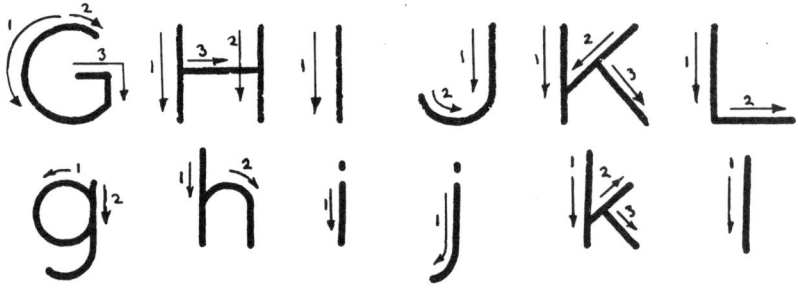

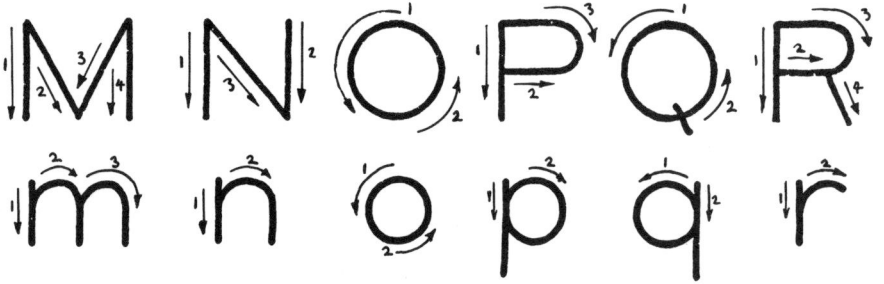

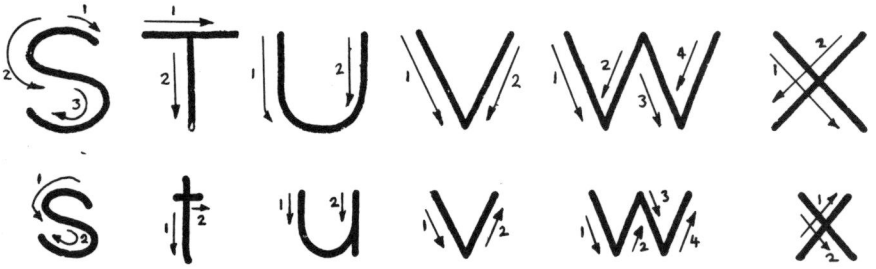

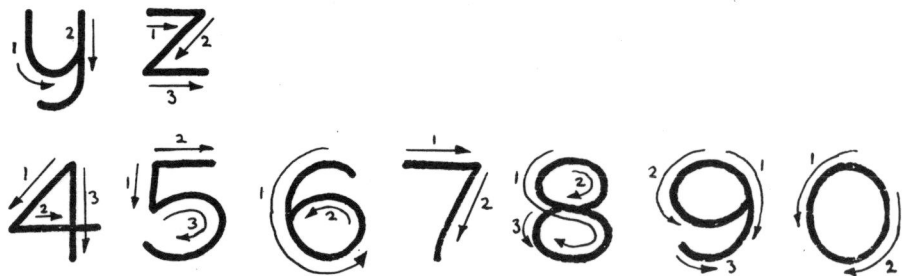

Routine: (Nos 1-6 may take you several days or a few minutes. It doesn't matter which.)

1.   Go over all the letters with your finger once or twice, just to explore.
2.   Choose the letters that make your first and second names.
3.   Copy them, trace them or get someone else to write them on to a piece of paper or an exercise book. They need to be big, the same size as ours. Make sure you get the spaces between them right, and that they're all the right size. Also, that your tall and short letters are distinct — ruling lines like this will help:

tall bits — capitals

middle bits

base line

tails

John Ray

4.   Finger-trace those.
5.   Then practise them in pen. Write them as small as you want to for your writing. Do them slowly at first, then speed up.
6.   Next, do the same with your address. If it's long, do it line by line. Addresses should look like this:

Name. Johnny Smith
House No. . . . . 29 Apple Grove
Town. London
Postcode WC1V 8QT

7.   Do the same with other names or addresses you need or want to write.
8.   Choose words from Part 5 of this book. They're mainly in joined-up writing, but that doesn't matter. In fact, it's a good thing to start doing that right at the start.

Part 3: **Speeding up**

How fast is normal?

Before you decide whether you need to speed up or not, you'll need to know how fast 'normal' writers go. And that's difficult, because, of course, everyone's different. Not only that, they write at different speeds for different purposes — very quick for scribbled phone messages or notes, slowly for letters to the bank manager. And the faster you write, the less tidy it becomes! On the other hand, if you write too slowly it's hard to remember what you wanted to say, so that's no good unless you're copying something out. And if it's dead slow your writing may look rather childish. There is a happy medium. I've put down what I think it is after the next activity.

When do you write fastest and why?
When do you write slowest and why?
Ask a few other people these questions. Do they all say much the same thing? Or is it all a matter of taste?

Here's what Jenny said:

> I write fast when I'm in a hurry – to dash off a note to someone, write down a message or something to remind myself of something. Or writing down something I don't want to forget, like a good idea. And writing down something which is easy to write, like a shopping list I'm going to read myself.

I write slowly when I would really like to be doing something else and can't really think about it because I'm not in the mood. So it's just an effort. Or when I'm trying to be terribly careful. And my writing's at its ugliest, and I get the worst hand-cramps when I'm copying something out. That's the most difficult kind of writing.

For me the answer is I write quickest when I'm doing my first draft, and slowest when I'm copying out the last one — the one that's going to be legible for someone else. People who know my writing laugh when they hear I'm writing this book — they've seen my first draft efforts (when I'm too lazy to write it out again).

The first draft is very important — it's the time you're thinking about what to say, not what it looks like. And you need to write fast, even if you stop every few minutes to think — otherwise you'll lose your thread. So here are some more questions to help you decide whether you still need to use this part of the book:

1. Do you write so slowly that you forget what you were thinking of saying, and keep having to start again?
2. Do you write so quickly that you can't even read it yourself?
3. Do you write fairly fast, but get worried about how untidy it is, so you find it an ordeal and can't really get down to it?

If the answer to 1 or 2 is 'yes', stay here! IF NOT, go on to p. 36.
If the answer to 3 is 'yes', go on to p. 32. IF NO, stay here.

Check your times

Here's an exercise that will tell you how fast you write. After you've done it you can check against the 'normal' times given below. But don't feel they are necessarily *right*. They're intended as a guide. I got them by taking the average speeds of seven people I regard as 'normal' writers. You'll see that there are two sets of times, one for right-handed and one for left-handed, since they usually write more slowly.

In your sloppiest, fastest hand, write 'God save our gracious queen' five times. DON'T WORRY ABOUT THE SPELLING. This is your private hand, you don't have to show it to anyone. Words can be spelled any way you want them to be. Time yourself, and write the time down in the bottom right-hand corner of the page. Don't use five lines, just carry on along each line till you get to the end. Here's an example.

God sve a gracan queen God see a queen, queen god sve a graning queen god sve an gramin queen god see a graue queen.

3 secs

In your neatest hand, do exactly the same thing. Try and make sure the spelling is right. If there are any words you're not sure of, copy them. This kind of writing is mainly for copying anyway. Time yourself. Write the time in the bottom right-hand corner of the page. Here's an example.

God save our gracious queen God save our gracious queen God save our gracious queen God save our gracious queen God save our gracious queen God

5 secs

And here are some examples of 'normal' writers' fast and slow writing:

19.6 *My hands make light work. May hands make light work. May hands make light work.*

34.6 *Many hands make light work.*
Many hands make light work.
Many hands make light work.

26

Exercises to help you speed up

There's a lot written about *reading* faster, and there are a lot of tricks that can help you do it. But, in the end, as psychologist Frank Smith points out, the great secret of fast reading is — to read faster!

Well, it's the same with writing. In the end it's a question of your attitude — you probably write slowly *because* you're being extra careful. You need to let your hand *take off*. Or maybe you haven't done much writing, so your hand tires quickly. If that's the case, make sure you practise for a few minutes (two or three is enough) several times a day, every day.

These exercises follow on from each other. When you can do the first one easily, go on to the second. Once you can do that, go on to the third, then the fourth (which carries on and on till you've had enough!).

1. *Signature*
Write out your first and last names as though you're signing a letter. Speed up till you can write them in five seconds or less (add a few seconds for really long names. Englebert Humperdinck can be allowed eight seconds at least!). It doesn't really matter if anyone can read your signature, though it's nice if they can.

Examples:

2. *The light touch*
You may be pressing too hard with your pen, and slowing yourself down that way. Try and find out how lightly you can press for it still to work. Try other kinds of pen.

   Draw a line across the page. Start heavy on the left and get lighter till it's as light as possible, like this:

(Insert line)

Do it a few times. Then write your signature as lightly as you can. Add a few words.

Do a few really light lines:

_____

_____

_____

When you can do a line right across the page in two seconds or less, go on to exercise 3. (It doesn't have to be straight.)

3. *Address*

Do the same with your address as you did with your signature in exercise 1. But you'll have to be slower as it must be legible. See how fast you can write it before it turns into a scribble. Time yourself. Practise for two minutes at a time, as often as you can, for one week. Then compare your time. It should be better.

4. *Use the key words*

Choose four key words from Part 5, p. 32. Choose the style you like, and join the letters you want to join. Find the most efficient way of joining them — either ours, or a better one of your own.

Do this exercise with each one:

1. Write the word down slowly.
2. Experiment with the light touch. How heavily do you want to write? (It may depend on your mood. If you're in a bad temper, use thick paper!)
3. Now try and speed up. Notice what bits of each word slow you down. Practise them. If you're leaving letters unjoined you'll need to practise getting them the right distance apart.
4. When you're ready, start timing yourself. See if you can halve the time it takes you to write one word, in one week.
5. Go on doing it till you run out of words. Then get some more, from Part 5, or anywhere.
6. Notice the way you write your fast words. Make sure you always write them fast in your 'real life' writing too. You should find other words are also getting faster.
7. If you haven't got a pen and paper handy, practise by FINGER TRACING on a table, a steamy window, your (or someone else's) knee (or whatever). For more on that *see* p. 21.

Part 4: **Mixed-up capitals and small letters**

A lot of people think that capital letters are neater than small ones. The impression is strengthened by the fact that so many forms demand BLOCK CAPITALS ONLY. And it's true that capitals are sometimes easier to read, but not because they're capitals. It's because you have to write them slowly and carefully. It's hard for anyone to join up capitals, and joining up is only useful for speeding up. Saying, 'BLOCK CAPITALS ONLY' is a way of saying 'WRITE SLOWLY AND CAREFULLY BECAUSE IF YOU DON'T WE WON'T BE ABLE TO READ IT!'. If you write neatly and clearly in small letters, the person reading the form won't mind at all. But this impression — that capital letters are somehow better than small ones — is one of the reasons some people mix them up. 'If in doubt, use a capital' seems to be a rule of thumb among unconfident writers. It's a bad rule. It stops you learning to write fast and efficiently, and it makes your writing look inconsistent and immature. So if you have this problem, here is a routine to help sort it out.

1. Look through your work. Notice which words have mixed-up capitals and small letters.

2. If there are a few letters you always write as capitals, choose some words which contain those letters and jot them down in the space below

3. Work on one word at a time. For each word: turn to p. 21. and choose a style for each capital you want to make small. Try several. Choose the one you like the look and feel of best.

4. Write the word in your new style. Write it big enough to fit between the lines as shown.

tall bits
tails

I must give you the glue

5. Finger-trace and practise as explained on p. 21.
6. Compare your performance at each word after 1 day; after 1 week; and (if you remember) after 1 month.

Date	Words with unwanted capitals	1 day	1 week	1 month

Unwanted capitals: if it's the grammar . . .

Perhaps you have this problem because you don't know when capitals should be used. Here are some ways to help you find out:

1. (a) *After full stops*
    Read a short piece in a newspaper. Don't take any notice of the reading, just mark each place where there's a full stop. After every full stop there should be a capital letter.

    (b) *What's a full stop for?*
    I once heard a teacher say 'A full stop is a blob you put when you've come to the end of what you're saying.' That seems to me to be exactly right. Try reading the piece out loud to someone. Or listen to them reading it to you. How do you 'read' a full stop? What does it tell you about the way the piece is read?

2. *After question marks (?) and exclamation marks (!)*
    Question marks and exclamation marks are just special full stops: one is used after a question; the other is used whenever the writer feels like it. If you want to find out more about exclamation marks, find the ones I've used in this book and see if you can work out why.

3. *The first letter of a name*
    The first letter of any name — people, places, brand names (John) (London) (Persil) — is always a capital letter.

4. *Quote marks*
    In between two lots of quote marks when they mean someone is speaking (' ') the first letter is a capital.

    Quote marks tell you when someone is supposed to be speaking. It's a way of using punctuation to control the reader's imagination. Quote marks tell the reader 'You must now imagine someone talking out loud.'

5. *Other places*
    There are probably other places where capitals are used. If you find one, try and work out why. (It could be a mistake though, so be careful.)

Every day choose one short piece from a newspaper and notice where three capital letters are used. Work out why.

Part 5: **You write fairly quickly but rather badly**

On the following three pages you'll find lists of words for you to practise writing. Each word is presented in several different ways. CHOOSE THE WAY THAT'S MOST COMFORTABLE FOR YOU. There's no need for us all to write the same. These exercises are to help you notice the details in *your* writing that need to be improved. They are *not* a model for you to try and copy. Because this is a printed book, our 'handwriting' examples are drawn by artists. Most people cannot write as well as that — most people don't get paid for it!

We offer you *the choice* of which letters to join to which others. You don't have to join everything to everything else. Hardly anyone does, it's too hard. To look 'mature' you should join some up, but only the ones that come easily to you.

The routine for practice

1.   Do one page at a time. Start anywhere you like. Choose the style you like best. Decide which letters you will join up. (Try several, and feel free to change your mind.)

2.   'Finger-trace' the first word: that is, run over it with your forefinger and get the *feel* of how the word is formed. Notice your finger going up, down, round, etc.

3.   Jot the word down with your pen on a piece of paper. Try and make it as much like the original as you can, but still in *your* writing. Notice how the bits all fit together. The exact shapes don't matter.

4.   Speed up a bit. Then, as you write normally, concentrate on that word whenever it crops up. Watch it gradually improving.

5.   Finger-trace it on your knee, on your desk, in the bus, anywhere, whenever you have a moment. Try and picture it in your mind's eye as you do it. It's all practice!

The words

and	with	again	January	thirteen
he	you	another	February	fifteen
in	about	because	March	twenty
was	before	good	April	thirty
it	call	found	May	forty
of	came	school	June	fifty
that	can	thing	July	hundred
to	come	under	August	thousand

all	could	very	September	tomorrow
all	could	very	September	tomorrow
all	could	very	September	tomorrow

be	did	work	October	yesterday
be	did	work	October	yesterday
be	did	work	October	yesterday

at	should	writing	November	house
at	should	writing	November	house
at	should	writing	November	house

but	like	complain	December	how
but	like	complain	December	how
but	like	complain	December	how

one	little	satisfactory	one	were
one	little	satisfactory	one	were
one	little	satisfactory	one	were

for	much	sincerely	two	no
for	much	sincerely	two	no
for	much	sincerely	two	no

had	must	yours	three	1
had	must	yours	three	9
had	must	yours	three	)

have	right	Dear	four	a
have	right	Dear	four	a
have	right	Dear	four	a

him	she	manager	five	darling
him	she	manager	five	darling
him	she	manager	five	darling

his	some	faithfully	six	child
his	some	faithfully	six	child
his	some	faithfully	six	child

not	their	Avenue	seven	children
not	their	Avenue	seven	children
not	their	Avenue	seven	children

on	this	Crescent	eight	condition
on	this	Crescent	eight	condition
on	this	Crescent	eight	condition

one	there	Road	mine	thank
one	there	Road	mine	thank
one	there	Road	mine	thank

said	where	Close	ten	Ltd.
said	where	Close	ten	Ltd.
said	where	Close	ten	Ltd.

they	here	Sir	eleven
they	here	Sir	eleven
they	here	Sir	eleven

we	other	Madam	twelve
we	other	Madam	twelve
we	other	Madam	twelve

Part 6: **Setting out a letter**

Dear Reader,

How to set out a letter

I am writing to tell you that half the neatness of any writing is in the way it's set out. If you set out a letter well, it looks good even if no one can read it. This is how it's done:

1. *Business letters*

Your address
```
21  Nott End
Meldrell
Royston
Herts
SG8  6WR
```

Date [28 June 1982

```
H.D. Symes & Co
Fast Works
Elphinick
Lenies
NW3  PQR
```
Firm's address

Dear Sir/Mr X ——— 1st paragraph

Thank you for your letter of 21 June. I am pleased to note that the parts I ordered will soon be available. I would be most grateful if you could let me know when these are despatched so that I can arrange for them to be collected from my local railway station.

I look forward to hearing from you.

2nd paragraph

Yours sincerely
faithfully

Ann Turner] Signature

2. *Personal letters*

   Same, except you don't put their address in. And you aren't confined to 'Yours sincerely' or 'faithfully' — you can put 'Love', 'Hate', 'See you', 'May the curse of the Pharoahs descend on you' . . . anything.

83 Blackfriars Street,
Wrexham

10/4/82

Dear Martin,

   Many thanks for putting us up over the weekend — we had a really great time. I hope you recovered in time for work!

   I've a horrible feeling I nicked your toothbrush! Hope the teeth haven't fallen out as a result!

   You must come up to see us sometime, and sample the local brews. Give me a ring when you have a spare weekend.

Regards,

John

NOTES:

NOTES:

NOTES: